Unlocking the Mysteries of Membership Decline in Freemasonry

Kyle Wilson

DEDICATION

CONTENTS

Introduction: The Decline of Freemasonry

Freemasonry has a long and storied history, dating back hundreds of years. At its core, Freemasonry is a fraternal organization that is based on the principles of brotherhood, charity, and truth. Through its teachings and rituals, Freemasonry aims to make better men out of its members, helping them to become more virtuous, charitable, and ethical individuals.

However, over the past few decades, Freemasonry has experienced a significant decline in membership. The reasons for this decline are complex and multifaceted, with no single cause that can be identified as the root of the problem. In this chapter, we will explore the factors that have contributed to the decline of Freemasonry, and examine some of the challenges that the organization is facing today.

One of the key factors that has contributed to the decline of Freemasonry is the changing social landscape. Society as a whole has undergone significant changes over the past few decades, with many people becoming more isolated and disconnected from their communities. This has had a profound impact on the fraternal organizations like Freemasonry, which rely on a sense of community and brotherhood to function. With fewer people participating in community organizations, it is no surprise that Freemasonry has seen a decline in membership.

Another factor that has contributed to the decline of Freemasonry is the changing nature of work. With many people working longer hours and having less time to devote to extracurricular activities, organizations like Freemasonry have become less of a priority. Additionally, many people today are more focused on their individual pursuits, rather than on community-building and charity work. This has made it more difficult for Freemasonry to attract new members who are interested in its core values and principles.

Technology has also played a role in the decline of Freemasonry. With the rise of social media and other online platforms, people are increasingly able to connect with others virtually, rather than in person. This has made it more difficult for organizations like Freemasonry to build a sense of community and brotherhood among its members.

Moreover, the public perception of Freemasonry has also changed over the years. While Freemasonry was once viewed as a respectable and reputable organization, it has come under scrutiny in recent years, with some people questioning its motives and practices. This negative perception has made it more difficult for Freemasonry to attract new members and maintain its relevance in the modern world.

The decline of Freemasonry is a complex issue that cannot be attributed to any single factor. Rather, it is the result of a combination of social, economic, and cultural factors that have impacted the organization over time. In the following chapters, we will explore these factors in more detail, and examine some of the solutions that are being proposed to address the decline of Freemasonry.

The Historical Context of Freemasonry's Decline

Freemasonry has a long and rich history, dating back to the late 16th century. Its origins are shrouded in mystery, but it is believed to have evolved from the stonemason's guilds of medieval Europe. Freemasonry spread throughout Europe and eventually made its way to America in the early 18th century, where it quickly became a popular fraternal organization.

Despite its early success, Freemasonry has experienced a decline in membership in recent decades. This decline can be attributed to a number of historical factors, which we will explore in more detail below.

One of the key historical factors that has contributed to the decline of Freemasonry is the rise of secularism. In the early days of Freemasonry, the organization was closely tied to religion, with members required to believe in a Supreme Being. However, as society became more secular and religion lost its grip on people's lives, this requirement became less relevant. This led to a decline in the number of people who were interested in joining Freemasonry, as the organization's religious ties became less important to them.

Another factor that has contributed to the decline of Freemasonry is the changing social landscape. In the past, Freemasonry was closely tied to the upper classes, with many of its members being wealthy and influential individuals. However, as society became more democratic and egalitarian, this social hierarchy began to break down. This led to a decline in the number of people who were interested in joining

Freemasonry, as the organization's elitist image became less appealing.

The rise of alternative forms of entertainment and leisure activities has also played a role in the decline of Freemasonry. In the past, Freemasonry was one of the few social outlets available to men, particularly in rural areas. However, as other forms of entertainment, such as sports, movies, and television, became more widely available, Freemasonry became less of a priority for many men.

Another historical factor that has contributed to the decline of Freemasonry is the changing nature of work. In the past, many men worked in jobs that were physically demanding and required long hours. As a result, they had less time and energy to devote to extracurricular activities like Freemasonry. However, as the nature of work has changed, with many jobs becoming less physically demanding and offering more leisure time, people have become less interested in joining fraternal organizations like Freemasonry.

Finally, the negative public perception of Freemasonry has also played a role in the organization's decline. While Freemasonry was once viewed as a respectable and reputable organization, it has come under scrutiny in recent years, with some people questioning its motives and practices. This negative perception has made it more difficult for Freemasonry to attract new members and maintain its relevance in the modern world.

The decline of Freemasonry can be attributed to a number of historical factors, including the rise of secularism, the changing social landscape, the rise of alternative forms of entertainment, the changing nature of work, and the negative public perception of the organization. While these factors have contributed to the decline of Freemasonry, they also present opportunities for the organization to adapt and evolve to meet the changing needs of its members and the broader community.

Understanding the Root Causes of Membership Decline

As discussed in the previous chapter, Freemasonry has experienced a decline in membership over the past few decades. While there are many historical factors that have contributed to this decline, it is also important to examine the root causes of membership decline in order to develop effective strategies for reversing this trend.

One of the root causes of membership decline in Freemasonry is a lack of relevance. Many potential members may not see the value in joining an organization that they perceive as outdated or irrelevant to their lives. Freemasonry must work to demonstrate its relevance to potential members, highlighting the ways in which it can enrich their lives and provide opportunities for personal growth and development.

Another root cause of membership decline is a lack of understanding of what Freemasonry is and what it stands for. In order to attract new members, Freemasonry must effectively communicate its values and mission to the broader community. This may involve engaging in outreach efforts, such as hosting public events or partnering with other community organizations, in order to build awareness and understanding of what Freemasonry is and what it can offer.

A third root cause of membership decline is a lack of diversity. Freemasonry has traditionally been a male-only organization, which has limited its appeal to women and non-binary individuals. In order to attract a more diverse membership, Freemasonry must work to become more inclusive, welcoming people of all genders, races, and backgrounds.

A fourth root cause of membership decline is a lack of engagement among current members. Members who do not feel engaged or connected to the organization are less likely to recruit new members or participate in events and activities. To address this, Freemasonry must work to create a sense of community and belonging among its members, providing opportunities for socializing and networking as well as personal growth and development.

A fifth root cause of membership decline is a lack of leadership and organizational structure. Without strong leadership and effective organizational structure, Freemasonry may struggle to attract and retain members. To address this, Freemasonry must prioritize leadership development and ensure that its organizational structure is designed to support growth and sustainability.

A sixth root cause of membership decline is a lack of innovation and adaptation. Freemasonry must be willing to evolve and adapt to meet the changing needs and interests of its members and the broader community. This may involve embracing new technologies, exploring new areas of focus, and experimenting with new approaches to recruitment and engagement.

Understanding the root causes of membership decline in Freemasonry is essential to developing effective strategies for reversing this trend. By addressing issues related to relevance, understanding, diversity, engagement, leadership, and innovation, Freemasonry can position itself for long-term growth and sustainability. By taking a proactive and collaborative approach to these challenges, Freemasonry can continue to thrive and evolve in the 21st century.

The Role of Technology in the Decline of Freemasonry

Technology has played a significant role in shaping modern society, and Freemasonry is no exception. Over the past few decades, technological advancements have transformed the way we communicate, socialize, and connect with others. While technology has brought many benefits, it has also contributed to the decline of Freemasonry in several ways.

One of the primary ways in which technology has contributed to the decline of Freemasonry is through changes in communication. In the past, Freemasons would meet in person to discuss important matters, share ideas, and build relationships. However, with the rise of digital communication, many members have turned to social media, email, and other online platforms to connect with one another. While these platforms can be convenient, they often lack the personal touch and sense of community that in-person meetings provide.

Another way in which technology has contributed to the decline of Freemasonry is through changes in leisure time. With the rise of smartphones, streaming services, and other digital entertainment options, many people have become more sedentary and less likely to participate in social activities. This has made it more difficult for Freemasonry to attract and retain members, as many people may prioritize their digital entertainment over participating in lodge activities.

A third way in which technology has contributed to the decline of Freemasonry is through changes in society's values and interests. While Freemasonry has a rich history and tradition, many of its values and teachings may not resonate with younger generations who prioritize individualism, self-expression, and instant gratification. Additionally, as society becomes more secular, the religious and spiritual aspects of Freemasonry may be less appealing to potential members.

Despite these challenges, technology can also be a powerful tool for revitalizing Freemasonry. For example, digital communication can be used to build connections and foster a sense of community among members who may not be able to meet in person. Social media can also be used to raise awareness of Freemasonry and its values, as well as to attract younger, tech-savvy members.

In order to harness the potential of technology for the future of Freemasonry, it is important for the organization to embrace innovation and adapt to the changing needs and interests of its members. This may involve exploring new communication platforms, experimenting with online and hybrid meetings, and leveraging digital tools to enhance engagement and participation.

Technology has played a significant role in the decline of Freemasonry, but it also has the potential to be a powerful tool for revitalization. By embracing innovation and adapting to the changing needs of its members, Freemasonry can position itself for long-term growth and sustainability in the digital age.

The Demographic Challenge: Attracting Younger Members

One of the most significant challenges facing Freemasonry today is attracting and retaining younger members. While the organization has a rich history and tradition, many younger people may perceive it as outdated or irrelevant to their lives. In order to remain relevant and sustainable for future generations, Freemasonry must find ways to appeal to younger members and adapt to their changing needs and interests.

One of the key reasons why Freemasonry may struggle to attract younger members is a lack of diversity and inclusivity. Historically, the organization has been dominated by older white men, which may make it difficult for younger people from diverse backgrounds to feel welcome or represented. In order to overcome this challenge, Freemasonry must actively work to promote diversity and inclusivity at all levels of the organization. This may involve creating programs or initiatives that specifically target underrepresented groups, as well as promoting a culture of openness and acceptance within lodges.

Another challenge in attracting younger members is the perception that Freemasonry is overly secretive or exclusive. While the organization's secrecy may have been a source of intrigue in the past, younger generations may view it as unnecessary or even suspicious. To overcome this perception, Freemasonry must find ways to be more transparent and open about its activities and values. This may involve providing more information about the organization on its website or social media, as well as creating opportunities for nonmembers to learn more about Freemasonry in a low-pressure, non-threatening environment.

A third challenge in attracting younger members is the perception that Freemasonry is overly traditional or rigid in its practices and beliefs. While tradition and ritual are important aspects of the organization, they may not appeal to younger generations who prioritize individualism and creativity. To address this challenge, Freemasonry must find ways to adapt its practices and beliefs to better align with the needs and interests of younger members. This may involve exploring new forms of ritual or incorporating more contemporary themes into lodge activities.

In addition to these challenges, Freemasonry must also find ways to adapt to the changing technological landscape. As younger generations become increasingly reliant on digital communication and entertainment, Freemasonry must find ways to integrate these tools into its activities and outreach efforts. This may involve creating social media accounts for lodges, hosting online events or meetings, or developing mobile apps that make it easier for members to stay connected and engaged.

Attracting and retaining younger members is one of the most significant challenges facing Freemasonry today. To overcome this challenge, the organization must actively work to promote diversity and inclusivity, be more transparent and open about its activities and values, and find ways to adapt its practices and beliefs to better align with the needs and interests of younger members. Additionally, Freemasonry must find ways to integrate technology into its activities and outreach efforts to remain relevant and engaging in the digital age. This will be vital in connecting with younger generations who find this as their main way of communicating with others.

The Role of Women in Freemasonry: A Key to Growth?

This will be the most controversial section of the book for many freemasons. But the fraternity is structured to rule out roughly 50% of the world's population just by gender. To look for growth this might be something that needs to be revisited. Women have been excluded from participating in Freemasonry as members for centuries. However, this exclusion may be a hindrance to the growth of the organization, as it prevents women from contributing their skills, perspectives, and talents to the group. In recent years, some lodges have begun to explore the idea of admitting women as members, and this has led to a renewed discussion of the role of women in Freemasonry.

Historically, Freemasonry has been a male-only organization. However, in recent decades, many lodges have begun to admit women as members. This change has been driven by a number of factors, including changing societal attitudes towards gender roles and the desire to attract new members to the organization.

One argument for admitting women into Freemasonry is that it would allow the organization to tap into a new pool of potential members. Women make up approximately 50% of the population, and many are highly educated and engaged in their communities. By excluding women from membership, Freemasonry is potentially missing out on a large group of talented and committed individuals who could contribute to the growth and success of the organization.

In addition, admitting women into Freemasonry could help to address some of the organization's current challenges. For example, many lodges are struggling to attract and retain younger members, and admitting women could make the organization more attractive and welcoming to younger generations who value diversity and inclusivity.

Another argument for admitting women into Freemasonry is that it could help to modernize and update the organization. As society has changed, so too have the expectations and needs of members. By admitting women, Freemasonry could adapt to these changes and become more relevant and engaging to a wider range of people.

Of course, there are also those who argue against admitting women into Freemasonry. Some argue that the organization's traditions and rituals are based on an all-male history, and that admitting women would fundamentally alter the nature of the organization. Others argue that admitting women would lead to conflicts and divisions within lodges, and that it would be difficult to integrate women into a male-dominated culture.

Despite these concerns, many lodges have begun to explore the idea of admitting women as members. Some have created separate lodges for women, while others have integrated women into existing lodges. These efforts have been met with varying levels of success, but many members believe that admitting women is essential to the long-term growth and success of Freemasonry.

In conclusion, the role of women in Freemasonry is a complex and controversial topic. While there are arguments both for and against admitting women as members, many members believe that it is essential to the growth and success of the organization. By tapping into a new pool of potential members and adapting to the changing needs and expectations of society, Freemasonry can remain relevant and engaging for generations to come.

Addressing the Issue of Diversity in Freemasonry

In recent years, the issue of diversity has become increasingly important in society, and Freemasonry is no exception. The organization has long been seen as exclusive and exclusive to a particular demographic, namely white, male, and middle-aged. However, in order to remain relevant and successful in the modern world, Freemasonry must address the issue of diversity and strive to become more inclusive and welcoming to people of all backgrounds and identities.

There are a number of reasons why diversity is important for Freemasonry. Firstly, in a rapidly changing society, it is essential to be able to adapt to new and different perspectives. By embracing diversity, Freemasonry can tap into a wider range of experiences, knowledge, and perspectives, which can help to enrich the organization and make it more relevant to a wider audience.

Secondly, diversity can help to address some of the current challenges facing Freemasonry, such as declining membership and the need to attract younger members. By becoming more inclusive and welcoming to people of all backgrounds, Freemasonry can create a more vibrant and diverse community, which can attract new members and help to sustain the organization into the future.

Finally, promoting diversity is simply the right thing to do. As a society, we have a responsibility to treat all individuals with dignity and respect, regardless of their background, ethnicity, gender, or sexual orientation. By promoting diversity within the organization, Freemasonry can help to create a more just and equitable society, which is a core value of the organization.

There are a number of steps that Freemasonry can take to promote diversity within the organization. Firstly, it is important to actively recruit and welcome members from a wide range of backgrounds and identities. This can be achieved by reaching out to different communities, creating partnerships with organizations that serve diverse populations, and actively promoting the benefits of membership to a wider audience.

Secondly, it is important to create an inclusive culture within the organization. This can be achieved by promoting diversity and inclusion at all levels of the organization, and by creating policies and practices that support diversity and inclusivity. This can include things like sensitivity training for members, creating diverse leadership teams, and establishing a zero-tolerance policy for discrimination or harassment.

Finally, it is important to recognize and celebrate the diversity that already exists within the organization. This can be achieved by creating opportunities for members to share their stories and experiences, promoting cultural events and celebrations, and creating a sense of community and belonging for all members.

The issue of diversity is essential for the long-term success and relevance of Freemasonry. By actively promoting diversity and inclusivity, Freemasonry can tap into a wider range of experiences and perspectives, attract new members, and create a more just and equitable society. While there are challenges to promoting diversity within the organization, it is essential that Freemasonry take the steps necessary to become a more inclusive and welcoming community. Not just welcoming diversity, but actually the process of seeking diversity and making others aware the fraternity has a big tent.

Building Stronger Lodge Communities: The Importance of Fellowship

At the heart of Freemasonry lies a sense of community and brotherhood. The organization was founded on the principles of mutual support, kindness, and fellowship, and these values continue to be central to the organization today. However, in a world where people are increasingly busy and disconnected from each other, it can be difficult to maintain a sense of community and fellowship within the lodge. In order to build stronger and more resilient lodge communities, it is essential to prioritize fellowship and create opportunities for members to connect with one another.

The benefits of fellowship within the lodge are manifold. Firstly, fellowship helps to create a sense of belonging and connectedness, which is essential for the wellbeing of members. By providing opportunities for members to connect with one another, the lodge can become a place where members feel valued, supported, and appreciated.

Secondly, fellowship helps to build stronger and more resilient communities. By creating strong social networks within the lodge, members can provide mutual support in times of need, and work together to achieve common goals. This sense of community and brotherhood can be particularly important during times of crisis, when members may need extra support and encouragement.

Finally, fellowship can help to attract new members to the organization. Many people are drawn to Freemasonry because of the sense of community and fellowship that it provides, and by creating a strong and vibrant lodge community, the organization can attract new members who are looking for a sense of connection and belonging.

There are a number of steps that lodges can take to promote fellowship and build stronger communities. Firstly, it is important to create opportunities for members to connect with one another outside of regular lodge meetings. This can include social events such as dinners, barbecues, and picnics, as well as volunteer opportunities and community service projects.

Secondly, it is important to create a culture of openness and inclusivity within the lodge. This can be achieved by promoting respect and kindness among members, and by creating a space where members feel comfortable sharing their experiences and perspectives.

Finally, it is important to prioritize fellowship within the lodge, and to recognize its importance in creating a strong and resilient community. This can include creating fellowship committees within the lodge, which are responsible for planning and organizing social events and activities, as well as promoting fellowship and connectedness among members.

Fellowship is essential for building strong and resilient lodge communities. By prioritizing fellowship and creating opportunities for members to connect with one another, lodges can create a sense of belonging and connectedness among members, build stronger social networks, and attract new members to the organization. While there are challenges to promoting fellowship within the lodge, it is essential that lodges take the steps necessary to create a strong and vibrant sense of community and brotherhood within the organization.

The Importance of Education in Attracting and Retaining Members

One of the core principles of Freemasonry is the pursuit of knowledge and wisdom. As such, education has always been an important aspect of the organization. However, in order to attract and retain members in the 21st century, it is essential to place an even greater emphasis on education, and to create meaningful opportunities for members to learn and grow within the organization.

There are several reasons why education is important for attracting and retaining members. Firstly, education can help to create a sense of purpose and meaning for members. By providing opportunities for members to learn and grow, the lodge can become a place where members feel challenged and engaged, and where they can pursue their intellectual interests and passions.

Secondly, education can help to attract new members to the organization. In a world where people have access to endless information at their fingertips, many people are looking for opportunities to deepen their knowledge and understanding of the world around them. By offering meaningful educational opportunities, the lodge can become a place where people can engage in lifelong learning and personal growth.

Finally, education can help to retain members by creating a sense of connection and shared purpose within the organization. By providing opportunities for members to learn and grow together, the lodge can create a sense of community and brotherhood, and help members to feel valued and appreciated.

There are several steps that lodges can take to promote education within the organization. Firstly, it is important to create a culture of learning within the lodge. This can be achieved by promoting the importance of education and intellectual curiosity among members, and by creating opportunities for members to share their knowledge and expertise with one another.

Secondly, it is important to provide meaningful educational opportunities for members. This can include lectures and presentations on a wide range of topics, as well as workshops and discussion groups that allow members to engage with the material in a more interactive way.

Finally, it is important to make education a central part of the lodge experience. This can include creating educational committees within the lodge, which are responsible for planning and organizing educational activities, as well as promoting the importance of education within the organization.

Education is essential for attracting and retaining members in the 21st century. By creating a culture of learning within the organization, providing meaningful educational opportunities for members, and making education a central part of the lodge experience, lodges can create a sense of purpose and meaning for members, attract new members to the organization, and retain members by creating a sense of connection and shared purpose within the organization. While there are challenges to promoting education within the lodge, it is essential that lodges take the steps necessary to create a strong and vibrant educational culture within the organization.

The Role of Mentorship in Member Retention and Growth

Mentorship is a powerful tool that can be used to foster growth and development within any organization. This is particularly true in the context of Freemasonry, where mentorship has long been recognized as a key component of the organization's structure and values. In this chapter, we will explore the importance of mentorship in member retention and growth, and provide practical guidance on how lodges can implement effective mentorship programs.

The importance of mentorship in member retention is a critical component of member retention within Freemasonry. New members often experience a sense of isolation and uncertainty as they navigate the complexities of the organization, and without the guidance of experienced members, they may quickly become disenchanted and disengaged.

Effective mentorship programs can help to mitigate these challenges by providing new members with a sense of connection and support. By pairing new members with experienced mentors, lodges can create a sense of community and brotherhood that encourages members to remain active and engaged within the organization.

Moreover, mentorship can help to ensure that new members are fully integrated into the lodge community. Mentors can help new members to understand the customs and traditions of the organization, introduce them to other members, and provide guidance on how to navigate the various roles and responsibilities within the lodge.

In addition to its role in member retention, mentorship is also critical for member growth and development. By pairing new members with experienced mentors, lodges can create opportunities for members to learn from one another, share ideas, and develop new skills and perspectives.

Effective mentorship programs can also help to foster a sense of accountability and motivation among members. By setting goals and providing regular feedback, mentors can help members to stay focused on their personal and professional development, and to make progress towards their goals.

Moreover, mentorship can help to ensure that members are fully engaged and invested in the organization. When members feel valued and supported, they are more likely to take on leadership roles and to contribute their time and talents to the organization. This can lead to a stronger and more vibrant lodge community, and ultimately to increased growth and success for the organization as a whole.

<u>Implementing Effective Mentorship Programs</u>
In order to be effective, mentorship programs must be carefully planned and implemented. Some key steps that lodges can take to create effective mentorship programs include:

1. Establishing clear goals and objectives for the program
2. Identifying and training potential mentors
3. Developing a system for pairing mentors and mentees
4. Providing ongoing support and training for mentors
5. Evaluating and adjusting the program as needed

Moreover, it is important to create a culture of mentorship within the organization. This can be achieved by promoting the importance of mentorship, recognizing and rewarding successful mentors, and providing opportunities for mentors to share their knowledge and expertise with one another.

Mentorship is a critical component of member retention and growth within Freemasonry. Effective mentorship programs can help to create a sense of community and support for new members, foster growth and development among members, and ultimately lead to increased success for the organization as a whole. While implementing effective mentorship programs requires careful planning and execution, the benefits for both individual members and the organization as a whole are well worth the effort.

Creating a Positive Public Image of Freemasonry

The public perception of Freemasonry has long been a subject of concern for members of the organization. Despite the many positive contributions that Freemasonry has made to society, there are still many misconceptions and stereotypes that persist in the public consciousness. In this chapter, we will explore the importance of creating a positive public image of Freemasonry, and provide practical guidance on how lodges can effectively communicate their message to the public.

The Importance of a Positive Public Image

A positive public image is critical for any organization, and this is particularly true for Freemasonry. In order to attract new members and build strong relationships with the broader community, it is essential that the organization be perceived in a positive light.

Moreover, a positive public image can help to dispel many of the misconceptions and stereotypes that persist around Freemasonry. By clearly communicating the organization's values and contributions to society, lodges can help to build trust and credibility with the public, and encourage greater understanding and acceptance of the organization.

Creating a Positive Public Image

Creating a positive public image requires a multi-faceted approach that involves both internal and external communication strategies. Some key steps that lodges can take to create a positive public image include:

1. Emphasizing the organization's values and contributions to society: Lodges should clearly communicate the values and principles that guide their work, and emphasize the positive contributions that they make to their communities.
2. Engaging with the broader community: Lodges should actively engage with the broader community by participating in community events, volunteering, and partnering with other organizations to promote shared goals.
3. Developing a strong online presence: In today's digital age, it is essential that lodges have a strong online presence that reflects their values and mission. This includes maintaining an informative and engaging website, as well as an active presence on social media.
4. Promoting transparency and accountability: Lodges should be transparent in their operations, and provide regular updates on their activities and finances. This can help to build trust and credibility with the public, and dispel any misconceptions or stereotypes that may exist.
5. Building positive relationships with the media: Lodges should actively seek out opportunities to engage with the media, and work to build positive relationships with journalists and other influencers in their communities.

Creating a positive public image is critical for the success of Freemasonry. By clearly communicating the organization's values and contributions to society, engaging with the broader community, and promoting transparency and accountability, lodges can build trust and credibility with the public, and dispel any misconceptions or stereotypes that may exist.

While creating a positive public image requires a sustained effort over time, the benefits for both individual lodges and the organization as a whole are well worth the investment.

The Role of Philanthropy in Attracting Members

Philanthropy has long been a core value of Freemasonry. The organization's commitment to giving back to the community has helped to establish its reputation as a force for good in society. In this chapter, we will explore the role of philanthropy in attracting and retaining members, and provide practical guidance on how lodges can leverage their philanthropic efforts to build stronger relationships with their communities.

The Importance of Philanthropy

Philanthropy plays a critical role in Freemasonry's identity and mission. By giving back to the community, lodges demonstrate their commitment to the principles of charity and benevolence that are at the core of the organization. Moreover, philanthropic efforts can help to build trust and credibility with the public, and create opportunities for lodges to engage with their communities in meaningful ways.

Attracting Members through Philanthropy

Philanthropy can also be an effective tool for attracting new members to the organization. By demonstrating the impact of their charitable efforts, lodges can create a sense of purpose and meaning for potential members, and provide a tangible way for them to get involved in their communities.
Some key strategies for attracting members through philanthropy include:

1. Highlighting the impact of philanthropic efforts: Lodges should clearly communicate the impact of their

philanthropic efforts, and provide opportunities for members to see firsthand the difference that they are making in their communities.

2. Creating opportunities for members to get involved: Lodges should provide a range of opportunities for members to get involved in philanthropic efforts, from volunteering at events to participating in fundraising campaigns.

3. Partnering with other organizations: Lodges can leverage their philanthropic efforts by partnering with other organizations that share their values and mission. This can create opportunities for collaboration and networking, and help to expand the reach and impact of their charitable work.

4. Building relationships with potential members: Philanthropic efforts can also be a powerful way to build relationships with potential members. By engaging with them in the context of community service and giving back, lodges can create a sense of camaraderie and shared purpose that can help to attract and retain members.

Retaining Members through Philanthropy

Philanthropy can also play a key role in retaining members. By providing meaningful opportunities for members to get involved in charitable efforts, lodges can create a sense of belonging and purpose that can help to keep members engaged and committed to the organization over the long term.

Some key strategies for retaining members through philanthropy include:

1. Providing regular opportunities for members to get involved: Lodges should provide regular opportunities for members to get involved in philanthropic efforts, and ensure that these efforts are meaningful and impactful.
2. Recognizing and rewarding members for their efforts: Lodges should recognize and reward members for their contributions to philanthropic efforts, whether through formal awards or simple expressions of gratitude.
3. Building a culture of giving: By emphasizing the importance of philanthropy and giving back to the community, lodges can build a culture of giving that encourages members to remain engaged and committed to the organization.

Philanthropy plays a critical role in Freemasonry's identity and mission. By leveraging their philanthropic efforts, lodges can attract and retain members, build stronger relationships with their communities, and create meaningful opportunities for members to get involved in charitable work. While philanthropy is just one of the many tools that lodges can use to attract and retain members, its impact and importance cannot be overstated. By continuing to prioritize and emphasize philanthropy, lodges can help to ensure the ongoing success and growth of the organization.

Effective Marketing Strategies for Freemasonry

In today's fast-paced, digital world, effective marketing strategies are essential for any organization seeking to attract and retain members. Freemasonry is no exception. In this chapter, we will explore some of the most effective marketing strategies that lodges can use to attract and retain members, from building a strong online presence to leveraging social media and targeted advertising.

Building a Strong Online Presence

In today's digital age, a strong online presence is essential for any organization seeking to attract and retain members. This includes having a modern, user-friendly website that provides information about the organization, its values and mission, and the benefits of membership. Lodges should also consider leveraging social media platforms like Facebook, Twitter, and Instagram to reach a broader audience and engage with potential members.

Some key strategies for building a strong online presence include:

1. Developing a user-friendly website: Lodges should invest in developing a modern, user-friendly website that provides information about the organization and its mission, as well as resources for potential members.
2. Engaging with social media: Lodges should leverage social media platforms to reach a broader audience and engage with potential members. This includes regularly posting updates and content, responding to comments and messages, and running targeted ad campaigns.

3. Utilizing search engine optimization (SEO): Lodges should ensure that their website is optimized for search engines, making it easier for potential members to find them online.
4. Providing online resources: Lodges should provide online resources for potential members, such as FAQs, testimonials from current members, and information on upcoming events.

Leveraging Social Media

Social media is a powerful tool for engaging with potential members and building a sense of community among current members. By leveraging social media platforms like Facebook, Twitter, and Instagram, lodges can create a sense of camaraderie and shared purpose that can help to attract and retain members.

Some key strategies for leveraging social media include:

1. Regularly posting updates and content: Lodges should regularly post updates and content on social media platforms, including news and events, photos and videos, and member testimonials.
2. Responding to comments and messages: Lodges should actively engage with members and potential members on social media platforms, responding to comments and messages in a timely and professional manner.
3. Running targeted ad campaigns: Lodges can run targeted ad campaigns on social media platforms to reach potential members in their local communities.
4. Encouraging member engagement: Lodges should encourage members to engage with each other and the

broader community through social media, by sharing updates and photos, commenting on each other's posts, and participating in online discussions.

Targeted Advertising

Targeted advertising is another effective marketing strategy that lodges can use to reach potential members. By leveraging digital advertising platforms like Google Ads and Facebook Ads, lodges can target specific audiences based on factors like age, location, interests, and behavior.

Some key strategies for targeted advertising include:

1. Identifying target audiences: Lodges should identify target audiences based on factors like age, location, interests, and behavior, and develop tailored messaging and content for each audience.
2. Utilizing digital advertising platforms: Lodges can leverage digital advertising platforms like Google Ads and Facebook Ads to reach target audiences with tailored messaging and content.
3. Tracking and analyzing results: Lodges should track and analyze the results of their digital advertising campaigns, using data to optimize future campaigns and improve ROI.

Effective marketing strategies are essential for lodges seeking to attract and retain members in today's digital world. By building a strong online presence, leveraging social media, and utilizing targeted advertising, lodges can reach a broader audience and engage with potential members in meaningful ways. While marketing is just one of the many tools that lodges can use to attract new members it is only effective when balanced with other recruitment methods.

Overcoming Internal Conflict and Division

Freemasonry is an organization that prides itself on unity, brotherhood, and mutual support. However, like any organization, Freemasonry is not immune to conflict and division. This chapter explores the importance of overcoming internal conflict and division in order to maintain the strength and integrity of the organization.

Internal conflict and division can arise from a variety of sources, such as differences in opinion or personality clashes. Whatever the source of the conflict, it is important for Freemasons to address the issue head-on and work together to find a resolution. Failure to do so can lead to a breakdown in trust, loss of membership, and damage to the reputation of the organization.

One effective way to address internal conflict is through open and honest communication. Members should feel free to express their opinions and concerns in a respectful manner, and leaders should be open to listening to and addressing these concerns. It is also important to establish clear policies and procedures for handling conflicts so that everyone knows what to expect.

Another effective strategy for overcoming internal conflict is through mediation and conflict resolution. Mediation involves a neutral third party who can facilitate communication and help parties find a resolution to their differences. This approach can be particularly effective in situations where emotions are running high, and communication has broken down.

Leaders within Freemasonry have an important role to play in addressing internal conflict and division. They must be willing to listen to all parties involved, remain impartial, and work towards finding a resolution that benefits everyone. This may involve compromise, but it is essential for maintaining the unity and strength of the organization.

Finally, it is important to acknowledge that conflict and division can also arise from external factors, such as changes in society or political climate. In these situations, Freemasonry must remain true to its values and principles, while also adapting to changing circumstances. By remaining united and focused on its core values, Freemasonry can overcome external challenges and emerge stronger than ever.

Internal conflict and division are challenges that all organizations face, including Freemasonry. By addressing these challenges through open communication, conflict resolution, strong leadership, and a commitment to core values, Freemasonry can overcome internal conflicts and emerge even stronger and more united than before.

A Call to Action for the Future of Freemasonry

Freemasonry has a rich and storied history, but it also faces significant challenges in the present day. The decline in membership and the need to adapt to changing societal norms are just a few of the challenges that Freemasonry must confront. However, with the right approach and a commitment to its core values, Freemasonry can overcome these challenges and continue to thrive for generations to come.

In order to achieve this, it is important to recognize the need for change and take action. This means being open to new ideas, embracing diversity, and adapting to the needs of a changing world. It also means recognizing the importance of strong leadership, open communication, and a commitment to education, mentorship, and philanthropy.

One key area where Freemasonry must focus its efforts is in attracting younger members. This requires a concerted effort to appeal to younger generations, including embracing new technologies, creating more inclusive and welcoming lodge environments, and offering programs and activities that ap-peal to a broader range of interests and backgrounds.

Another important area of focus is in building stronger lodge communities. This requires a commitment to fellowship, mentorship, and education, as well as a willingness to address internal conflicts and promote unity and mutual support among members.

Additionally, Freemasonry must continue to work towards diversity and inclusivity, both within the organization and in the wider community. This means addressing issues of gender, race, and ethnicity, as well as creating a more welcoming and inclusive environment for all members, regardless of their backgrounds or beliefs.

Finally, Freemasonry must continue to promote its core values of brotherhood, charity, and truth. By living up to these values and being a positive force in the world, Freemasonry can continue to inspire and uplift its members and the wider community.

The challenges facing Freemasonry are significant, but they are not insurmountable. By embracing change, promoting diversity and inclusivity, and living up to its core values, Freemasonry can continue to thrive and serve as a beacon of hope and inspiration for generations to come. The future of Freemasonry is in our hands, and it is up to us to seize the opportunities before us and build a stronger, more vibrant, and more inclusive organization for the future.